"In this supreme hour the Irish nation must, by its valour and discipline and by the readiness of its children to sacrifice themselves for the common good, prove itself worthy of the august destiny to which it is called."

*1916 Proclamation*

# ON CORKSCREW HILL
## STEPHEN MURRAY

**salmon**poetry

Published in 2013 by
Salmon Poetry
Cliffs of Moher, County Clare, Ireland
Website: www.salmonpoetry.com
Email: info@salmonpoetry.com

Copyright © Stephen Murray, 2013

ISBN 978-1-908836-52-6

COVER IMAGE: "Holde's Hares" by *Róisín Coyle* – www.roisincoyle.com
COVER DESIGN & TYPESETTING: *Siobhán Hutson*
*Printed in Ireland by Sprint Print*

*Salmon Poetry gratefully acknowledges the support of The Arts Council*

For Sean Kier

Who placed a book of giant words into a pair of tiny hands

# Acknowledgments

Thanks especially to Ronan Considine and Brendan Murphy for their help and advice. To Jessie and Siobhán for their continued support and tireless work. To my sister Jenny who I simply haven't written a poem worthy of dedicating to her. To Dave Lordan and Neil McCarthy for teaching me the art of love and leather. To Bethan Hope-Evans for being Bethan. To Noeleen Kavanagh, Kernan Andrews, RTÉ's *Arena*, Olaf Tyaransen, Dimitra X, to Sheila Kier, Mick Geraghty, and all my Irish, Greek and Egyptian families. To all the people I have forgotten.

And of course Róisín Coyle.

# Contents

# Burren Sunset

*for Ann Kenny*

Winter burned her sunset here

against the bare black bones

of ghastly trees she pointed

a silhouetted finger and cursed

the summer's youthful radiance

then fell ashamed to wind-scraped knees

her sky in full crepuscular blush

beyond karst and leaden landscapes

after the tearful tantrum

of the wild Atlantic rain.

# A Graduation in Templemore

Uniform hats flung skyward

    into clouds of violently feckless

        ubiquitous blue.

Scattering brain cells abandoned

    to the East Munster wind

like confetti at the wedding

    of the wolf to the ewe.

# At Pollathomais, County Mayo

*for Sarah Clancy*

*[It was a] political donation for my personal use.*
FORMER IRISH TAOISEACH BERTIE AHERN

Battle blue riot batons drawn like shillelaghs
set to scalp the skulls of slipper clad secondary school teachers
and farmers in Aran wool with ladies wrapped-up like tea cosies
crash to stone and sod and bleed into the rain soaked muck
upon land cultivated on the bones of war and famine dead
by oceans fished forever through wild centuries of winter.

Came skulking down long, winding lanes in blacked out balaclavas
from bog to brine to pastured glebe backed by Bertie's boys in blue
to play Punch and Judy with the fortunes of hard working folk,
fisherman and their weathered wives, with lobster pots and trawling sons,
all puppets to the pantomime villainy of the Oireachtas.
Bought and sold to the behemoths of oil and gas and thirty five thousand
of your silver worth of liquor, gift wrapped at the doorstep of the law.

This one's on the department boys from the right honourable jailbird
former Minister of Hyenas raising his cracked whiskey glass
to Templemore's finest new recruits of clockwork rangers.
Just pull the string or wind them up and point them where you want them
with a wink and a nod to the New Model Army of the Garda Síochána
from the pin-striped kleptocrats of Bord na Móna.

# On Wolfe Tone Bridge, Galway

A crowd has gathered on Wolfe Tone Bridge.
In a tightly knit huddle of whispering shadows.

Death's Angel has come
to raise Lazarus from his silt bed.

Great red and white skull-headed lord of bent steel
crowned in a halo of whirring scimitar blades.

A cormorant spreads ceremonial wings
as neoprene midwives deliver us this day's
diabolical messiah.

Stillborn again before the iron star of morning,
where rushes give way to coffin and cradle

Whispers fall hushed to the pardon of light.

# Bird Man Spawns

*For Brian Phelan*

> *'Therefore it is God's decree*
> *Bare to the world he'll always be.'*
> "Sweeney Astray", SEAMUS HEANEY

### 1.

I, king cock, post-hatch, half wild, part man, beak fed
Crowed upon the dawn of the roost of the high-stool-born,
Womb-shell cracked in blazing red
Last known heir to a barbed wire throne in a kingdom of spit
Who was hushed up proper by a bishop's limp crook
To the froth-born yak of my eloquent mush
And nailed by the claw-hooked hand of each wing
To a shattering stained glass notion of gospel
The devil's own pack, half jokers and jacks,
A straight card flush, part magic trick stroke truth
Strung-up by the neck in the sheds of my youth
And condemned for the out-of-line cut of my jib
To live in the liminal gloom of the chatterbox darkness
Tied up in knots by slivers of iridescent light
To the hoot of the moon in the conjuror's night
By the whispering, whispering
Whispering world.

### 2.

I am who am you who is they who is us
Who is molten cerebral beneath the skull's crust
Half cut, part gay, translucent, silent, still, come what may
Who hovers in midair, brass bollock bare and brazen as fuck
Beneath the frenzied spotlights of the raving sun
Naked and deranged in candy bar towns besprinkled with visions
That burst into wildfire lynched upon pitchforks

17

Trembling in asylums of unsullied flesh
In black debased basements caught in the tangle
Of a fine spun cobweb of shuddering chills
I shrank out of sight in a bottle of pills
And bled from the ear to the nightingale's tune
Who could fly off your cliffs to the song of your grief
Then perch upon branches, light as a leaf
In the gathering, gathering
Gathering storm


3.

I who can ride on the blustering steeds
Of the tongue-bitten wind until bitter words bleed
From the fresh open wound of my jabbering mouth
Blabbering absurd incantations of naught
I post upon pedestals grinding my teeth as you stand
At the pulpit or kneel on your penitent knees at the pews
To crucify Gods you would worship and whip
And then like a virus go spread the good news
Of your suffering souls condemned to restraint
Beloved by demons and cursed by the saints
To live in my head away with the birds
Yes it was I that taught them to sing
And I heard thunder clap in the silver-washed beat
Of a mid-May meadow-bound butterfly's wing
And was lost for a while in the wilds of myself
In a riddle of shadows that bulged from the walls.
Who was lead by the hand through the dark by the blind?
It was I of the muttering
Muttering, muttering mind.

4.

I who could fly with the shadows of dusk
Wept for the sun when the sun turned to rust
Who could see every world in the maddening clouds
Knew the lore of the crows for I taught them to talk
Who was picked up and worshipped in out-of-town town bars
And burned every love by the fire of the soul
That kindles the mind set ablaze in the stars
Thus was I judged in your hollowed-out eyes and confess
To the blessed congestion of what you believe
Is carved in the stone of your corpse-fed creed
Yes I confess, I confess, I confess.


5.

It was I who was tarred and then feathered
And hung upside down by the unbroken bread of my body
Left in the stocks of apostates and thieves
Where the red-necked, half-witted, deaf, dumb and blind
The thoughtless and flightless minstrels of misfit
Gathered to brand me the beadledom's leper
For displaying in full feather the wings of the mind.


6.

So I soared in my dementia on the keening of the wind
With the landscaped bludgeoned and the red sky skinned
I wailed at the flowering song of the shrub
I hooded the rook and bespeckled the dove
When the Cardinal cursed what the Morrigan blessed
I lay with the robin and reddened her breast
A fine holy madness to wreak amongst men
For the pennies they gathered to bury the wren
In the harrowing, harrowing
Harrowing muck.

7.

And here, at last, with our rainbows spent
I sang in the full plume of my bedlam
Like a lark in the nethers of the brimstone sun
And every colour of the world was a feather of the soul

So I sang to the hacked-out crescent of the haloed moon
To the adolescent seed of the gobdaw state
To the blue clad batons of the gombeen law
To the bone headed puppets of the amadán Dáil
And my song was a godless land without faith
That the fat of the land spat back in your face
And poisoned with sorrow the seed of your men
Piping my sickness from furrow to glen,
For I danced on your grave well before you were dead
And I spray painted red '*not right in the head*'
Then I skipped through your mirror and with a tip of my hat
I died in a dream and then never came back.

# Willy

*for Elaine Feeney*

I met Willy on a building site
in South West London.

We were labourers on a concrete gang.

He was 65,
      I was 20.

   And his smile was cut with a spade
   in the hard tan leather of his skin.
   His eyes were the windows of archers.
   His soul was a fortress within.

*Never work for the Irish*, he said,
   shifting his weight onto one hobbling leg.

Then he paused to rest on the handle of his shovel,
pursing his lips beneath the slits of his  eyes,
he fired a volley into the heart of the point.

*No one fucks their own like quite like us.*

*They wouldn't screw the English though,*
*Sure Paddy knows the English won't take it.*

He said it with a smile,
staring hard at the ground,
spitting tobacco and dust.

# Wake

Then sorrow stirred from its dark and silent slumber,
filling its chipped glass to the cracked rim,

it swallowed the wallowing world in one.

And every uttered word seemed wrong.

Each comforting hand misplaced.

We huddled together like a flock of torn shadows.

All Catholic and guilty as sin
since the moment of conception
till they lay us out

cold as drowned sailors.

So we drink like fish,
making cartoons of our waking grief.

And then we bury our tears with the dead.

# A Refusal to Mourn the Death
# by Fire of a Dublin Model

*"I shall not murder*
*The mankind of her going with a grave truth*
*Nor blaspheme down the stations of the breath*
*With any further, elegy of innocence and youth"*

DYLAN THOMAS


It is not that a life snuffed out
before the autumnal breeze of age
can breathe the elegant shades
of those to whom time comes swanlike
upon the still waters of privilege,
where all of spring's colours ripen
besprinkled in summer's labial verses
from leafy Dublin suburbs whose existences
are, by proxy, deemed more or less valuable
or worthy of our tears and our disgust than
that which crawls in the needle-teeming
rivers among the guttural swarms from
the tombstone streets of Ballymun or
Southhill or The Glen or wherever it is
that you press hard upon your pedal to pass.

It is more that the several tens or hundreds
of thousands of taxpayers funds used to fund
a public inquiry to finger the blame upon those
shadows we discard at the hostelry door could have
provided a hospital bed or a homeless shelter
or a helping hand or a therapist's salary or a two
or three-day break in the sun or a methadone fix
or an ear and voice or a friend at the end of a phone
in these dark ages of the eternal suicidal winter
to lift the bemoaned souls from these eternal dead-end streets

whose daily demise does not cause ripple or wave
upon the still waters of still privileged Ireland
and there will be no inquiries neither public nor private
for the myriad homeless, the sick and decrepit
whose lives by the thousand are not worth a headline
and much less still than one single more fashionable grave.

# On Serpentine Avenue, Bankcentre

1.

Two deranged twisted metal horns form a V.

An altar of martyrdom towered on all sides by marble.

Rectangular colonies of pathogen interfaced wayfarer eyes

an architectural palindrome scored into the flesh

of the young and oblivious with diamond cut blades

in underground laboratories by the stiff-collared acolytes

of Baphomet slouched behind cedar wood desks

upon Chesterfield armchairs commanding their hoards

of automaton drones to feed off those corpses you dredge

from your rivers, who drowned in the teardrops of children

whose futures are forfeit to the past. Then to toast their mojitos

on Fridays in Slattery's, in that other place,

the one that is insulated and soundproofed.

That leafy world that exists outside of office hours

when the telephones lines go dead and the night turns cold.

The one just outside your window that stretches to the horizon

of whatever vista is framed by the parameters of your conscience.

2.

Yes, two metal demented claws form a V.

A victory for the devils that bought you and sold you

two fingers in a *fuck you* salute to your young

a '*so what?*' to your sick, to your helpless and homeless

a shard from the splintered glass heart of a world

that fell from the sky to land at the black gates

of hell made on earth with a finger-light, feathery tip of the scales.

Great dreadnought of finance, run amok then aground;

bejeweled in debasement and beached upon the banks of a bluff

beneath azure parasols where the flotsam and jetsam of human decay

are washed away by the tide. Then into the storm in invincible bronze

with Flanagan's hare at the helm to rub salt

in the wound where your balls used to be.

For each solstice accosted and fingered by Balaam,

in the robes of the church that begat all you whored and bedazzled,

to toil in the dirt for the flags of your serfdom, with thanks everlasting.

Black monolith of glutton, great temple of Mammon

where the consecrated suffer the salvation of dogma

or *whatever it is that you're having yourself*

and the same again please for the rest of your life.

All that you wish for is spent and your dead are forgotten.

Your children long gone from the shores that right fucked them

like nobody else would have dared.


3.

For two steel sacrificial daggers form a V.

A wishbone in silver that cannot be broken

or shared by the masses yet plucked all the same

from the carcass of Eden the serpent's confession

for the efforts you made for your blossoming young

with your back to the wall, the blind gold of the sun

chased hard at the heels of your harlequin masters.

As sewage rose up through the pipes where you drank

your offspring grew sicker and froze in the snow

you begged for forgiveness to a little Miss Fortune Teller

Archangel chatterbots pinstriped in myriad headsets

with direct lines to God and virginal voices, pray with us, pray with us

for merciful Moloch to call off the hounds at the door

where you dragged your family's existence through fear

of the letter box snapping its jaw to bite off your fingers

in semi-detached mausoleums where you buried your dreams

in the nightmares of children, yet to be born.

So your screams fell dumb to the deafening roar

of a fusilier's song for twelve gold stars on a fuck you flag.

Now even your ghosts cannot spare you their penance

for there shall be no forgiveness for the debts of your conscience

or for the material endeavour of your synthetic soul.

# On O'Connell Street

The ridgebacks are rounding on O'Connell Street
On the heels of their haunches in pockets of shadow

Sucking John Player's in gaunt ashen doorways
Hollow eyed and hooded in the banners of Spartans

Bold as brass-bastards of nobody's King
Needle born riddles of silver-striped flannel and kennels flung open

To unleash the hounds of plutocracy's nightmare in tinker-silk slang
And the boys of last summer are all dead or gone

Where the unborn are cradled by juvenile wraiths
On riverside benches generations of junk starved degenerates

Marauding as sane in the garments of dead men
The claw-headed banged-up, the knocked-up and mad

Whose Fathers suffered hallucinations of spouse and were lured
And then legged it from black and blue sirens on roundabout islands

Sitting by chip vans to sing for a supper of smacks to the mouth
Or the blue throbbing vein of any old sailor

Where children ran wild and were weaned by hyenas
The bloody clenched fist of first daylight born in rich bitumen

Tattooed and toothless hook handed pushers
Push cocoons of hookers in hand-me-down prams

Walk wounded and drooling in unbuttoned silence
Branded and rounding in chemical clouds

Outside the burger chains that closed all the penny arcades
Then slipping like eels beneath unsettled concrete

To feed on the things you discard without blinking
Into gutters where we spit every word ever uttered

For the scamp-mannered ridgebacks to harvest the filth
Swept under the rug of our fragile decorum

In the tenement archives we shovel our shit
With our secrets as dirty incestuous.

# Surf Talk in Bundoran

And as for those men
whose words ping-ponged off walls of foam.

Heroic belly scratchers
great pouting chaps, hallelujahs of mankind
statuesque upon the elbows of Atlas.

In the rattle of whose heads
brains cells joust for territory
over oceans of skull space
vast and roaming wind-breaks.

Bronze words rip-curled into gold
insights spectacularly formed
breaking like white water
in the shallows of the blue-eyed mind.

# Accident and Emergency

Chewing on *fuck you, you cunt*,
in a cesspit of odorous dental decay

In a mouth hacked out full of blood,
liquor-swill and smashed-up tombstone teeth.

Knuckles caked in the shit of it all
sing under the evening star

of a sovereign ring.

Our Lord and Our Lady in silent prayer
beg for our forgiveness.

From a pulpit of bulging biceps
he swears to God he did nothing.

He swears it.

He swears on the life of his children.

# In Merlin Park Hospital

The walking wounded flank the walls
  where last year's posters spit free advice

and freephone helpline numbers
  ring out unanswered in unmanned offices.

Nurses at the gates of hell
  shepherd groaning paraplegics

into military formation out the door
  into the rain outside the orthopedics clinic

where the helpless and the broken limbed
  are propped-up upon the bayonets
  of crutches: Made in Britain.

Against the distant crack of German guns
  hollow voices boom rhetorical cannon fire

on Raidió Teilifís Éireann

landing like unexploded shells upon our Irish beaches
  from an invisible war demanding our children's

compulsory national subscription.

# Night Nurse

The night nurse has come

       in a cackle of shadows
       where pain's echo ricochets
       off daffodil walls demented
       in hallways lit up like a coffin.

              Where the broken are flung in
              the vestments she stitched from
              the morphine's delirium, choked
              at the stem of your blossoming pain.

She is chewing the bitter cane of
her years spent with lepers forcing
a badly stitched smile from the wound
of her mouth full of bluebottle flies.

              Her flesh falls away as you
              beg for relief, half wound of a man,
              the ward of a lunatic, the skull of a
              clown with needles for fingers

Pursing her lips in a surgical gown,
the night nurse has come like a
mother that beats you and you smile
when her mouth twists into a scar

As she dresses your wounds with her spit.

# The Twelve Pubs of Christmas

The clowns of Yuletide have rolled into town
in well knitted motifs of polymer snowmen
a herd of wind-whipped, whisky-nosed reindeer
to the jingle bell jangle of lepers in Santa hats-
pot-bellied toy makers in last Christmas's jumpers.

Tossing good tidings with Jaeger-bomb greetings
*Merry Christmas me arsehole ye mistletoe whores.*
For the twelve pubs of Christmas threw open their doors,
with room at the Inn for you and your donkey
ye wise men who bare gifts that you stole from your children.

There'll be no silent night for the doctors on night watch
and the cost of your mirth will be counted in litter
in broken glass doorways by the ghosts of last Christmas
that your goodwill stepped over on the way out the door
yes the spirit of Christmas is screaming your carols.

And the valley of darkness is lit up like a tree.

# On Raven Terrace

*for Lisa*

I remember her best

           on Raven Terrace

it was Galway Pride

      in the summer '05

           on all fours led by the leash

strapped to the black leather

silver studded collar

      on her neck, she barked

at the hand

           that fed her on the ground

where she played puppy

        to the Dyke Queen of Swans.

There was pride in every smile

for the glitter on her skin

      soft as the bulb of an unspent tear

with a star on the button

      of her tickled-pink nose.

For the Galway sun came out that year,

      the sun came out,

           and shone.

# Habemus Papam

White smoke hushes
from the rooftops of the Sistine Chapel

Pale whispers billow in the darkness
of the Vatican-black night

In clandestine gardens love's abomination blooms
stolen kisses shimmer like spells

Shadows bulge in seminary halls
Gregorian chants echo off cold hallowed walls

At midnight a soprano's song swells like a secret
spent in blind conclaves of unbuttoned silence

A ferryman ferries the flight of swans
to shores awash with empty naggins and teenage tears.

While one final gulp of vodka and a fistful of pills
damns another rainbow soul to mortal sin.

*Deo dingus vindice nodus*[*]

[*] A knot worthy of God to untie

# Eucharist

*for Mick Geraghty*

Blessed art thou amongst sinners
Blessed the habit, the collar, the crown
the shroud and the veil
the boy on his bended knees
Blessed the silence of children.

*Take this, for this is my Body.*

Blessed the sanctimony of flesh
the shame of the queer
the shepherd and wolf
who seeks out the lost
the blood of the lamb that is spilt

*O Sacred Heart of Jesus, abode of justice and love,*
*have mercy on us.*

Blessed the fruit that is torn
from the tree the unwavering trust
and the hand to the knee
to the crotch to the mouth
Blessed the word against his against mine
against hers against theirs
against God's

*O Blessed Virgin, mirror of justice, pray for us.*

Blessed the seed of the rapist
the cloth of the pious
Blessed are those who walk in the
valley of darkness alone
Blessed the consecration of innocence
the word, the lie, the song
and the whisper

*Behold, the hour is at hand,*
*and the Son of man is betrayed.*

Blessed the Eucharist of unblemished youth
the penance, the cage of whatever is written
Blessed be they who suffer unto blindness
Blessed the fruit of thy womb
that poisons the blood from within

*Blessed art those who trespass against us*

Blessed art thou amongst sinners.

# Youth Defence

Putrefied visions crucified to billboards
wielded and wailed from the rank open wound

Of a head held high in confession and stigma
emboldened on articulated trucks parked outside

Dublin's Rape Crisis Centre. Seriously.

Then into the schools of your daughters
to sing the good Lord in the halls of a convent

And keep sacred the seed of your demons
that flowers and spawns legislation

still–born into gutters

By circus masters leading suicidal girls
to audition by panels of experts in clown suits

With stethoscopes poised upon six figure sums
to bury our Mothers in our God–given guilt

For the swift termination of the unborn truth.

# On Wine Street

On Wine Street today I saw a woman,
perhaps a darts player's wife, or a bad day for porn.
Maybe she was an art installation
or the emblem of chips.
She emerged from a crowd of pot-bellied stags
and hens gutter-fucked by curly cocked pigs.
She was squeezed into a toddler's corset,
crowned in the gold of Argos,
tattooed in varicose blue-
great Goddess of Egg.

A pioneer of female flatulence,
a hoarder of all the Benidorm cellulite,
she was flanked by beefed-up boyos on steroids,
body hair waxed down
to their suntan lotion-oiled skin,
pouting into the blacked-out windows
of souped-up Subarus.

And when she spoke she sang
in wondrous splayed and arcing syllables,
a great wingspan of words;
vast and flapping catastrophes of insight,
all the grammar of flamingos on glue.
It was something in slug-talk about defecating
in the back of a taxi and tipping the driver forty pence
cackling *Happy Fucking Christmas*
*you dirty Paki cunt.*

# On Fanore Strand

When the window's wound up
the windscreen steams

Your shocks pull tight
as the springs lock load

With the wipers doing ninety
as the wind groans hard

In the bosom of the Burren
on a black lace night

From the unbuttoned silence
slips a hot breath gasp

Thrashing in the darkness
to a tongue-tied rasp.

The hazard lights are flashing
in the accidental rain

As the lightning strikes the ocean
like a phallic silver vein

There's a thrash of pale limbs
in the Burren National Park.

The twisted flesh of sinners
spitting Pinter in the dark

Now all the cars are rocking
back and forth under duress

They worship at the altar
of their unclean flesh

The shapes of unknown bodies
are shifting in the fog

For the bold Atlantic swell is up
and growling like a dog.

# On Corkscrew Hill

*for Sheila and Tony Falco*

### 1.

On Corkscrew Hill a rolling bluff of silver clint carves
a neoglyph of ringforts etched by smiths of time

A slumbering golem, stonemason to the world turning iron
upon the anvil-hammered moonscape, opens an encumbered eye

To watch a hundred million years roll by in threes, where no two skies
the same are seen, fires of life are snuffed out one by one

The howls of wolves are swallowed by each waking moon
till none remain but the bones of bear picked clean by Razorbills

Blind stallions of the furnished deep from silent graves come bounding
in black clouds of Lesser Horseshoe Bats on Corkscrew Hill.

### 2.

On Corkscrew Hill Pearl Bordered Wings wane upon the Druid's Altar
and the Wood White Moth stalks the prehistoric night

Here the Blue Flowered Gentian springs impossible from grykes
and the Bloody Cranesbill embroiders stony dykes

The Redshank and the Warbler perch upon proud pedestals
and for the Common Sandpipe's turlough, a Black Hearted Raven's crone

For here silence has a heartbeat for the Pigmy Shrew and grub
and the Autumn Lady's Tresses sing amongst the Hazel Shrub

The hooves of time stick fast in rock and the Swan Maiden's silver wilderness
is combed beneath her Downy Birch on Corkscrew Hill.

3.

On Corkscrew Hill the maids of Moira Rua were hung
by the hair on their heads till dead with their breasts sliced off

And bled with fading Dedonites in graves that lined the boher
there to cut the throats of songbirds beneath Balor's fading sun

Then for seven streams of milk a fatted calf came overflowing
to raise the Forge of One-Eyed Lon from pastured rill to dust

Take these your bleeding maidens and the sharpened steel of Scotia
let the seven sons of lightning pluck your last green blade of grass

For here a bag of shekels bends the jagged backs of heroes
crooked as a hunchback on the hag of Corkscrew Hill


4.

On Corkscrew Hill an architect, a builder and a banker
a twisted manifesto, and an auctioneer's dark will

There is a Hole of Sorrows plundered in the shattered limestone
that the County Planning Officer built upon the Devil's Chair

Here the screaming wind has been seized upon by saints
and then buried in the hollows of the County Council's crags

By whose black endeavour sprang a hermitage for jesters
built of brick and mortar for the ghosts of Slieve na Glaise.

And pedalled plain as grubstakes by bootleg benefactors
both luxury and location are cut price on Corkscrew Hill.

5.

On Corkscrew Hill a winding road snakes to Lisdoonvarna
and a corporate Rumpelstiltskin spins a harpy's gold from clay

Where a British Leyland tractor at the pace of our long winters
rolls at the speed of cattle, chewing time like old tobacco

With Galway Bay upon the vista, hat in hand towards America
while all the way from China a tour bus disembarks

As the rising moons draws shadows o'er the fading lights of Aran
The West Awake no more to bare ill witness to the sun

And the tangled spindle silver stands wrought against the tempest
where the road winds its soft lament around the bluff on Corkscrew Hill.

# The Big Freeze

When the snow came
the world shimmered like a spell,
seemed to stop for a moment,
then resume in slow motioned silence.
Silence for one, solitary second.
Gradually the music started,
building faintly in the distance.
Like an ice-cream van
in a neighbouring estate.

Footsteps crunched like wrapping paper
crinkled in the room next door.

Cars rolled by at the speed of hedgehogs.

Engines whispered discontent,
songbird's song arced from bare black branches
like question marks concealed in quavers.

Doors threw open unleashed hoards
of brightly coloured Wellington boots
wrapped snug in woollen scarves.

Children tucked in mittens
screeched and snowballs flew
like falling stars and lovers loved
in huddled corners of warm breath,

Stolen kisses punctuated the cold in soft pink.

Old folk shuffled pigeon footsteps,
clutched red leashed choke chains,
trembling terriers with shocked fur
frozen in tartan getup whined.

Murmuring bus stops moaned of the twinkling cold,
with groaning hip joints and wrinkled smiles.
Invincible slippers gave birth to wriggling toes
beside open turf fires. Coughing
through red brick chimneys.

Midnight's doting moon
blew snowflakes like kisses
at the sleeping world.
News readers smiled.
Headlines sang incantations of snow.
The front page of *The Times*
showed a picture of a duckling on a frozen pond
and the snow was a promise that turned
our stony grey winter to diamonds.
For one shimmering moment
there was magic.

Real magic.

Then somebody's grandmother slipped
on the ice and the accident and emergency room
was a clatter of broken bones.
Our picture postcard winter turned,
snarling Siberian blizzard jaws snapped.
Storm force winds froze our smiles
till lips cracked and bled.
Coppers pipes burst, roads froze over.
The front page of *The Times*
screamed of *Carnage on the Roads*.
The wireless reported a tangled metal tomb
where a mother of three perished.
News readers tucked in their chins to speak with grave voices.
Across Europe the elderly froze in their cots,
airports grounded, schools closed,
cars pirouetted, abandoned
at one frame per second.

Sirens moving slower than heart beats in stasis
with not enough salt for the thaw
on an island surrounded by ocean
all water ran dry.
Ireland's Jester Kings lead the dance.
Yucca trees died and the last Silver Queen
bowed her grey branches and wept
her last dark purple flowers to the ground
then wilted to the frost.

And was gone in the morning,
forever.

# On the Kilmallock Road

A lantern is being snuffed out among the burnt-out,
boarded-up shipwreck of South Hill.

The last remaining troops from the front lines of education
are facing a Dublin firing squad.

Children on meds are stowed away
into crates marked in thick red ink.

Some are marked *the jailhouse*
others are not marked at all.

# The Rain

*In memory of Francisco Valenti*

First, the symbols on the wind
that sweep and crash on Galway shores,
and in the distance phantom fingers
scrape the surface of the bay.
Whipped as light as soft-brushed jazz
that lick the snare of Silver Strand
a drop on unsuspecting skin
trembles on the hawthorn leaf.
Braids the crystal cobweb spun
in beads of glass on household doors.
Raft spiders scurry into shelter,
misty skyline rainbows bloom
upon the spectral landscape born
till each and every droplet spilt
shall polka dot the cobbled stones
and drive the drinkers from the streets
with shoppers swept by gusts of doubt
huddled into Shop Street doors
with brollies blustered inside out.
And shaking from the tallest trees
as old and tall as time and space
came shafts of light upon the sod
to part the seas that fed the storm
and gazed upon the gaze of God
till all the rooftop typists type
a bursting bodhrán's brail of clouds
that corrugate the tinker's sky
to fill the pots on window panes
and ruffled angel's feathers hark
hosanna to the falling rain.
The rain upon the Burren
that cascades into the darkest caves
the turlough born to drown the plough

sailors slide across the bow
what tricks the salmon wets the fly
floods the wells and deepens streams
for rain is what the river dreams
of drowning men upon the backs
of stallions whose stampeding
torrents gallop into washed-out towns
the running sound of fiddles
trickles in between the weeping stones
invoking from the fossils
in the gleaming pebbles polished
pale and clean as old Milesian bones
abandoned upon beaches
sets the stage for sunshine
to be ambushed by
the archers of the rain.
The rain, the rain
that never ever misses
smothers each and every lover
in the landscape of its kisses
snuggled under eiderdown
or cotton soft white pillows
bodies warm to tender touch
from chimney tops love billows
on the oceans spiral spurs
the wild assault Atlantic squall
to drag the surfers in to surf
and send the whirlwinds in their mirth
to whip a frenzied drinker
to recite the stony soil of verse
and toast the beating heart of every footstep
trod that ever carved a path
through howling gales and sheets
that drive the stars of blazing neon lights
to fall like midnight's squandered gold
adorned in the blackest tar of gutters
in the darkest nights and booms

of booming thunder breaking heaven's heart in two
for nothing quite like lightning
let's you know that you're alive.
So when Monday morning's bus stop splash
is sniveled into tissues and teaspoons
stir hot whiskeys in old leather shoes and socks
soaked to aging bones are toasted by the embers
noses red as Wexford strawberries scrunch
when dogs are barking kettles whistle
berries fall from thorn and thistle
skies as grey as Claddagh swans
calls forth the ghosts of Sean Nós dancers
to clips their heels and call the stones
to chatter in the shaking ground
the legions of the ocean's drowned
come roaring in their majesty
to praise the sacred, supernatural, ghastly
romance of the rain.

# On Tirlan Farm

*for Shelagh*

On Tirlan Farm he showed me
how to build a soldier's shelter
out of branches intertwined with ferns
upon the mountain's side

And banging stones together
he threw up a clash of sparks from flint,
hurling flames upon the heather,
he lit a fire in childhood dreams.

He named each constellation
and put a poet's verse on every star
as he placed a book of poems
into a pair of tiny hands.

Whose giant's hands once thread
a fishing line through all my summers,
taught me how to build a secret den
out of old corrugated iron.

Who rejoiced in all my childish fears,
conquered with gruff baritones,
he scoffed at love yet kept its twinkle
burning in his eyes.

So I followed his bold footsteps
to where the mountain road was falling
into long abandoned quarries
where old railways use to run.

For he walked in boots twice the size
of my vanquished drunken father's
and with his hands upon my shoulders
told me no one was to blame.

For the misfortune of a drowning man
can smash a broken Mother's heart
overboard to where love's shanties
crash upon our shipwrecked shores.

But for catapults and arrows
carved by silver-flicked Swiss Army Knives
are the last form of survival
that a lad need ever know.

For on Tirlan Farm all boys are king
and every falling star's a secret
scrawled in silver ink
that only seadogs can decode.

Where waking nightmares come to pass
and in that sea of broken glass
we mutineered around the campfire
Beneath the cutlass of the moon.

And staring out as the last pirate ship
sailed towards the setting sun of youth,
we buccaneers waved goodbye to him
as Tirlan fell to time.

Now brooks that teemed with salmon
bleed the lead tears of dead colliers,
and the Ospreys builds their nests
on city bus stops far away.

And the only thing that's colder
than the bottom of a bottle,
is the tombstone of an armchair
before the television's snow.

For an empty nest is nothing more
than deadwood amongst the living
yet every broken feather
wields a quill with tales to tell.

And on the summit of that mountain
haunted by dismantled men
the frailty of our youth found strength
beneath his broken wing.

# Mountain Man

A man has come down from the mountain.
A man with coral skin.
Hollowed out caves house his eyes.
His tongue is a nettle
in a mouth full of sores.
He broods in the dark corners
of cavernous hostelries,
staring down the endless barrels
of bottomless pints of plain.

He smashes rocks
with great ogre's hands,
rips trees from their roots
with gargantuan troll arms.
He growls at strangers, sniggers
clenching club fisted knuckles,
thin lips chewing upon the bitter cane
of his long indignant years.

He spits *nigger* at the immigrants
*whore* at single mothers.
He stands to salute *Amhrán na bhFiann*,
and slaps the backs of men who laugh
and beat their wives.
A great man for his county.
A great man for Ireland.

A man has come down from the mountain.

A man that the mountain spat out.

# Coming Down in Stradbally

In the house that burnt,
a sunken garden folded in amongst fractured
splinters of a chaise longues and antique
cabinets, spilt diamonds and cracked china.

In amongst the shattered
crystal chandeliers, a broken dollhouse,
the hydra's fossilized corpse, a fragment
of paradise spilt and a harpies claw.

And in the claw a porcelain doll,
unbroken against the silhouetted skeleton
of a junk yard horizon, the night cremated
stiller than the altar of her ceramic smile.

And in her smile a silence
and in her silence an undiscovered priory
and in the priory his clandestine tread
following softly the ephemeral footprints of dust.

And in the dust his shadow lost amongst
refractions of colourless light, empty paths,
the ghosts of friends, the unattended grave
of tender moments, laughter's echo in flight.

And from each echo a horse drawn carnival of
brightly-coloured caravans, tarpaulins of skin
tattooed with the complete history of man and
womankind illustrated by gypsy hands.

And in each illustration the unfading ink
of their fingers, memories scored into
the flesh of time, unabating grassy verges,
the black river's white noise.

Their curtains of self thrown open,
revealing an angel of pure light, upon a stage
obscured by a cloud of dust, a freshly dug grave
a porcelain doll, a harpies claw and a screaming clown.

# Concerning Love and the Universe

Ask me again to ask the universe
for an answer.

Tell me how you are a creature of it

how you can hear its whisper.

Feel its heart beat echo in the
fabric of your skin its rhythm's
pulse in time with flickering
apertures of a distant light.

Tell me please, so I can hear
you utter it.

Now utter it.

Tell me so, about the universe
that I can tell you that I have never felt so present
in it
than when our two bodies came together
like we were the last two perfectly fitting cogs
in the machinery of all things.

I will tell you of those rhythms that echoed between us
beyond the physical or sublime.

Where two bodies collide in time and space and feel
the turning of the earth with each unfolding instant,
its orbit around the fevered sun, the rotating gears
in the time piece of the planets outside of which
the only other sensation in each singular moment
was the warmth of the stars on our backs.

Everything that was or could be
all that came to be or die all
that moved in the waltz of it all
did so by the slightest deliberation
of our hips

Tiny implosions
of perfumed breath burst
from the petals of your lips
giving birth to new dimensions
with every shudder of your body
and were gone

in the blink of a new born eye.

Where everything that ever existed or was imagined

was consonant in the symphony of our sex
and yes we were gods in each other's arms.

Each morning held its own angel before us
                        silently mouthing our names.


            The touch of our skin was as the palms
            of two hands coming together in prayer.

Now ask me again to ask the universe

            that I might be there to watch it
                        happen at the event horizon
            born by the parting of your lips.

Ask me for an answer and I shall tell you.

The light of the stars
that now warms your back
is dead a million years.

The space
in between our bodies
for every
infinitesimal moment
spent apart
is as cold

and as permanent

as love and death.

# Daithi Talks Art

*Fuck that shit*, he says

Adjusting his glasses at the bridge
of his nose

*I'd be overrun* says he

*Those fuckers from Shoreditch*
*in their shirts with their shoes.*

*Sure, I've no interest in them*

*I'd rather hang out*
*with 70-year-old transvestites*
*from Saint Petersburg.*
*Living on crystal meth with pierced eyeballs*
*and lanced scrotums*
*in bedsits of utter turmoil.*

*Making real art.*

# An Púca Sings the Sands of Time

When the sky gave birth to time
as the ships of men sailed in
I danced a gypsy dance for one
and crowned him puppet king.

Then turning into ocean wind
I whispered him a verse
he sang it like an elegy
and he spoke it like a curse.

It was I that gave Chú Chullain
the strength to slay the hound
and it was by my whisper
that Ferdia bought the ground.

Reaching deep into the earth
I grasped a nudge of gold
which glittered in the morning sun
for all men to behold.

When Patrick came to pray for you
I convinced you I was God
painting every sunset
with the crimson of your blood.

Appearing as a stallion
I was black as mortal pain
thunder was my charging hooves
the night sky was my mane.

Yes I'm the darkest instinct
when you choke upon a scream
the loving claw upon their skin
as your children softly dream.

When the Norseman purged the soil
and you swooned in bloody swells
I appeared before a holy man
in the burning town of Kells.

So I threw my druids tunic
over the black ink of the sky
and I dazzled you with lightening
as the Dark Ages plundered by.

When Cromwell came to wet his blade
as your bravest heroes fled
I bought you gifts where you lay
weeping in your beggar's bed.

A spell to find a twinkle
in the teardrops of your young
for you the golden Lyre of Pan
and a storytellers tongue.

Then appearing as the wolfhound
growling upon the Hill of Doon
I made my mischief in your flesh
and howled it to the moon.

For I'm the last song sailors sing
in the moments before they drown
an echo of what isn't there
from far beneath the ground.

When famine came I dressed
your corpses well for you to eat
and I bid the ships of Boston
to come begging at your feet.

And I sent your sons a sailing
to the New World's gilded shore
I sent them there to fight and die
for somebody else's war.

And I whispered to your youngest
with my breath of tempered rage
they sang my song in fire and blood
against the crown's tirade.

I taught them how to shadow dance
and speak in silent tongue
from war's unchartered darkness
where my revolution sprung.

So when all proud the King's horses fled
with all the proud King's men
I set your rifle's sights up north
and bid you fight again.

A silhouetted Balor
I transformed into a bull
black against the tan of dusk
with the moon's magnetic pull.

For I'm the hemlock in your Eucharist
in the church your sorrow built
and the flags you fight and die for
are the emblems of your guilt.

When the Tricolour was hoisted
your victories all were sung
it was I that taught you spectral pipes
and banged the phantom drum.

You sang of love that could not be
and you sang of endless war
but the song you loved the most was death
so I brought it to your door.

I whispered *Fenian rise for me*
*your country's hour is nigh*
so you blew Britannia limb from limb
into the London sky.

When you cleaved the lives of innocents
I played the forgiving priest
toward your hand soaked in blood
I held the hand of peace.

Appearing as a black bronze hare
upon the Merrion Road
I slaked myself upon your greed
and watched your world implode.

I sent the silver banker there
to underwrite the bill
with the heavy booted builder
who plundered Corkscrew Hill.

Yes I'm the hand that picked you up
just so I could watch you fall
I'm the chuckling goblin
in the alcoves of the Dáil.

I'm the secret that your churches
are too afraid to tell
The river's voice that calls to you
in your melancholy hell.

The twinkle in the barman's eye
the *sure you'll have one more*
the fist with which you beat your wife
the mischief that you whore.

For I'm the changeling changing,
a wild horned mountain goat
and while Jesus Christ may have your back –
the Púca has your throat.

# Wind Turbine

*for Tony Murray*

Angels from a timeless landscape

    Guide the ghostly ships of Danu

    Into harbours of dark enterprise

    To wake the souls of sleeping Gods

And whirl like spectral dervishes

    Draped on grey horizons, a kaleidoscope

    In druid white to steer Milesian minds

    To reach into the sulking soil and scatter

Erin's ashes into the cartwheels of the wind.

# Dreadnought

### 1.

I set her adrift today
imagined her to be a sail boat
adorned with fairy lights
floating gently into the night.

And for her howling wind
I turned fiction into song
of a gentle breath of wind
caught in moonlit silver sails.

When thunder cracked
I heard the echo of her voice
felt lightning singe my back
felling the apple tree I used to climb
which I imagined to be love.

### 2.

A bottle arrived today
washed up on the shore
the man who delivered it
said something about
serendipity which was
a word I had always wanted
to drop into conversation
but never had the notion
or the gall.

Inside the bottle was a parchment
browned by time or blood
or afterbirth or faeces or fingers.
It was sealed with wax and marked
with a man's thickset thumb print
rolled into a cigar. It stunk
of booze and tea and sweat
and cum and blood and chips.

I unrolled the parchment
and read it. The handwriting
looked just like my own
but it wasn't, Whoever wrote it
wrote with great force almost
tearing the paper, probably
gripping the pen with a clenched fist.
The note read:

I LOVE YOU


3.

The fire is warm
and it is beautiful.

Like a golden pocket watch.

A dancing serpent headed gypsy.

It is God's heart cracking black whips.

A lullaby to keep a burning child from waking.


4.

A pirate has come to these shores.
*It's serendipity* I say
dead chuffed with myself
and the townsfolk agree
for he is dressed all in white.

He has come here this pirate
to save all our souls
and all that he asks is that we beg on our knees
for forgiveness and flesh, on our knees

with hands together, pleading
begging, and I don't know
for what or for why
the townsfolk are worshipping him
maybe it is because he is dressed all in white
reckons he's back from the dead
*back from the pub more like it* I say
then he hits me with it
and my chakras gush blood
old wounds open at once
crawling with yellow maggots
so I leg it all peg legged,
heart strewn and broken in two
as I fast I can to the sea
cursing serendipity
and pirates in white.


5.

I set her adrift you see,
sunk my fairy boat bride
like a hoard of Blackbeard's booty.
I sunk her and sang
a curse on all Mothers,
a pox on your cradles.
A plague of flying lawnmowers
with whirring blades upon you,
may your chakras gush blood,
let the flesh eating hoards
at your children.


6.

And she was a landscape of kisses
The blossom of coffins in spring.
And she was the flag and the drummer
That bury their dead with a hymn.

7.

On the ocean bed no sail boat
no pirate's gold, no flickering lights
nothing, only darkness.

I found her here as I left her.
Teeth bared for battle,
swimming with slithering things.
Unseen or heard of secrets,
the ones you can feel on your skin
when pimples pop their heads up.
Torpedoed she was, done for, done in
sub-fathomed as a wet brain.
Where once bottles of bubbly
cracked off her bow,
songs burst into Roman Candles,
gunfire and song in her siren's death roll.
Now silence sank with her,
no sailor survived her.
I left her as I found her
shipwrecked and broken,
haunted by drowning men
as ever she was.


8.

I set her adrift today
and imagined her a sail boat.
I imagine her a sail boat
flickering fairy lights etc.

# White Tailed Eaglets Hatch in Mountshannon

*for Sally Coyle*

A fissure on the black sky

Of a secret universe cracks

To a rhythm of things without meter

Eternal things nestled

In a Moses basket of feather.

A golden beak and plume emerge

Swathed in new-born slime.

Birth blind, sacred, flightless necks

Stretch toward the yawning sun

To the rockabye lullabies that arc and swing

Upon the cradles of the Munster wind

And place impossible slippers

Upon the first forgotten footsteps

Of flight.

STEPHEN MURRAY was born in Ireland in 1974 and moved to London in 1975. His formative years were spent living with his mother and sister in Erin Pizzey's historic shelter for battered wives in West London. As a teenager, whilst living in a children's home, he was twice a runner-up in the W.H. Smith Young Writer of the Year Awards. In 2005 he was crowned Cúirt Grand Slam Champion. He has performed his work as guest reader at many of the world's most famous poetry venues. He currently lives and writes in County Galway where he works as director of Inspireland, teaching poetry and creative writing to young people across the country. This is his second collection, following 2011's *House of Bees*.